Dragging Nothing

Chance Freihaut

Presentation by *BookLeaf Publishing*

Web: www.bookleafpub.com

E-mail: info@bookleafpub.com

ISBN: 9789395950152

First edition 2022

DEDICATION

To the reader, thank you for your time. I hope it isn't wasted.

Sheepskin

Sheepskin, bleeding
Sheepish kin,
Starvation at thanksgiving,
Sinews on a stalk,
A shudder and I'm gone,
Hold back the sun,
Garden beetles don't run
They walk to their end
Name the day,
Make it personal,
Fall anywhere,
See what catches,
I won't.

I Was Driving

There's a red spot on the collar of my linen shirt
It stays there in the closet, in the dark
I don't think I'll wash it.

They pulled you from the car,
But they were dragging nothing.
I walked out and rubbed my head,
that's all.

I wanted to see you
But they had the bag all ready
But I saw enough
You're in there,
 a new cocoon,

It's spring now
You can come out,
I still have to wait,
You'll take me to the basement,
Show me how it's done,
Get that stain for good.

A burden that lightens

Fresh mud is more than dirt,
A spider web isn't just a home,
Those cracks aren't just broken,
It's getting hotter
Time is there watching,
Throw us a bone, hey?
I swear She's smiling,
What's not to love?
We're sitting on our homes,
Water says hello from the town over,
Can it get a little higher?
We're fighting for scraps.
Go on now
The chopper's here,
The kids still get a summer
The water's not bad
I'll just check the basement
I think I left something there.

To your right, over your shoulder

Green up to my neck,
You're nearly spoiled,
Fat, bloated,
The essence of ooze
is your name.

Gaunt but fresh,
A skull, vanitas in motion,
Remember it all again,
It wasn't just in spring,
The door was never open.

My friend Cal

Paper bag stuffed in the side of your Honda
civic,
Grease pooling, vinyl getting sticky,
MSG stuck to your fingertips.

Radio tuned to static,
Windows up, seat back,
Head peeled like a tuna can.

Was it your dad's?
I don't see you hunting quail.

Buckshot or slugs?
It wouldn't have made a difference.
You're spread out on the backseat now.

Moleskin in your breast pocket,
Pages all blank,
Couldn't you give us something?

Got your mom on the phone,
She's breathing, but that's it.
Why do I have to tell her?

Tanka for the Birds

6

The heron stands still
Two legs that never quiver
Living through its beak
Eyes from the past taste the air
Take flight winged pearl of silence

Midday dinner for the Insatiable

The water at China beach isn't the same as the water that flows out of my sink. Forget the ceaseless abyss and foam, forget the crabs that straddle rocks as they wash ashore, forget the call of the waves as they die into their predecessors. The water at China beach took me in and began to eat. The salt was there to clean the flesh, to sting and to seal, the sand, kicked into a storm of hard dirt, masked me in its torrent. A scream forced itself out and the ocean answered with its own. I only had one in me. The sea did not stop. A metronome for the trees, it called and called with its ceaseless rolls until I closed my eyes and took its voice away. Waves were no more, nothing started, nothing crashed. My legs were numb, and I could hear nothing but the din of horns from across the glass horizon. I could not stay in the buoyant womb forever. It would take me whole if I let it. When I opened my eyes, Her turbulent voice returned to the foam, to the lichen on the trees near the shore, to the rocks that never dried, and to the water that still chewed the fat I left it.

Give a yarn, my friend

Launching dust with your index,
Sending it to nothing
Gone now, dispersed, just a slice of air.
Your hand, softer than
The cherry wood it sweats into.
Palms pressing through,
squeeze but never close.
The paper's in your pocket,
The ink is running down,
Stains on your trousers,
Words went to the thread.

Get up there
That podium
That alter
Speak
Tell them all about me
Watch their eyes
Where do they go?
All the things I've done
All the things I said
All the things I am.

Can you give it a word, a name?
Or is it just so, just an impression,

Just the print I gave you and no one else.
See their eyes, see what I gave them,
Do you have it too?
Don't grieve, oh please,
What is this loss to you?

Cosmos Ex Nihilo

Stretched thin, hands on Orion
Toes dipped in the exosphere.
My lungs eat white dwarfs,
My belly, slow pulse,
A dune, black matter sand,
Solar eclipse through my femur,
Refracted into Saturn,
Spin its rings
Extra-terrestrial nausea.

My eyes, false spheres
Split from the stem,
New globes for the ISS,
And my skin,
Soft, putty for the sun
Take it all and run
Lap Pluto then come home,
Keep me taut.

When it comes,
Mass black vacancy,
Let it ride,
Watch its wrath,
Once it has a sliver
It has everything,

It doesn't pull,
Consummation is primordial,
Beyond the bang.

All this flesh of me
Not lost but gone,
Through the tunnel of ends,
The other side of unity.

Again, the stars rest,
My head the last to go,
Don't shout, don't fret,
Silence is not the killer,
Clothe me in obsidian,
Great cloak of
 the astral plane.

A sinner all the same

Get there and just stop
That's how it goes
Running, now you crawl.

Wide mouth taking all the bugs
Hurl them kids down
Chuck and spit

You're on the top
You earned it
You're gushing; you're leaking

It's stuck now
Under your nails
It pushes beneath your scalp

Gotcha
Gotcha
Go to confession

Find that release
Lay in bed
Your husband's lamp
Is never on

Clutch a cross
Talk to Him
Whisper then yell
He'll hear it all the same.

No Spoons

The man on the corner sells soup.
Two ladles, large and small.
Two bowls, just the same.
If you're late, you wait.
Two at a time, no chairs.
Stand and drink.
Listen to the trail of yesterday.
Drain your bowl and return.
He gives it to a small boy,
Some say he's his son,
Others say he's homeless,
To me, though,
He's just a boy with a duty,
Rinse those bowls down at the river
Scrub them with your dirty hands
Run back, run now, quick
Others are waiting.
Now I can dine
Now I can forget
Now is the only meal of my life
I have never really eaten before.

Simple Choices

The bog is narrow but long
Mud, slabbed like sandstone
Formed and fashioned
Created for containment,
Not walls but windows,
Reflect all you see,
A step is just a step
Forward is not where you want to be,
You know the end
He waits
It waits
All your delay
A party of one
Filled with all
You'll take it standing,
Slapped into the muck
Drift down into the wet
Fringe of the ego
Encapsulate then erase
Rebirth is surrender
And then
And then
Defile all imagination
Polluted but sparse
Repopulate your mind

This time, this time
Hope is tonic
The cut is not physical
Find that thread
Is it existence
Is it essence
Which should proceed?

Futility

17

Fissure, not a break
Threaded, silver screw
Oil runs the helix,
Churn and turn,
We'll seal it up good.
Don't mind the excess,
Just another chore,
And those droplets,
Those crystals,
Those loaded lanceolates,
Give them up,
They won't spoil.

Again, I go Today

Just failure
The repetition of necessity
Non-logical ending
Birthed from routine.
Done to oneself
Relentless clockwork
Stammered justification
Ignorance is fiction
I am the lie
Caesar or nothing
Close in on finitude
Crack my knuckles on it
Derelict, borne of
Weightless friction,
And diction, my choices,
Free to will them to purpose
And propose, might I know
That they fail me
Bound by their clarity
Escape into the unknown
And now I flounder
For there,
Without my words
I cannot crawl
Towards the
loop.

Untitled

If not spring, then when?
Today, limbs cry for their leaves.
Come, Mother, grace them.

Condemnation

Remember me like dry roast,
I was in and out
Nothing to wash me down.

And your dreams,
Spoken for us both,
Yet the trail was yours.

I am not the past
You know this too
Embedded, branded with you

Flagellation, peeled fruit,
Watch my nectar run
Grip the leather and go.

The clots will come,
Skin over skin,
Something whole again

Remorse is a spear
You wield it well
The spirit has left me

Find your patch and rest,

Examine the blade,
Last dredges of me.

Farewell is an understatement
The chance,
come and gone.

Redemption found Longinus,
Can it find you?

soirée à deux

22

The wine is running out
Pouring over your legs.
All over the floor,
It spells a sacred name.

On all fours,
We slurp,
We suck,
Cobblestone is so cold
The Bordeaux is served chill.

Retreat upstairs
Domestic canopy
The sheets are my veil
Gateways,
Gossamer REM.

Once, there was danger

I found a switchblade
behind the deli.

Handle of black lacquer,
The antithesis of a pearl.

The spring was young,
Eager to greet my thumb.

Double-sided steel
In case I wanted to choose.

I put it in my breast pocket
The cold metal warmed me.

Lunch break was over,
I could smell my glee.

I sliced provolone
And porchetta.

I cut parmesan with a bandsaw,
It split open like a grapefruit.

All the while, I felt it,

Itching to open up.

A terror took my hands
The spring whispered softly

If not now, then later,
Let me be.

I lied about a cigarette,
Ran out to the dumpsters.

Just one flick
Just one flick

The handle gripped me,
My skin looked so dark.

My wrist let out a snap,
Completing its cycle.

This knife I saw was clear,
A reason for leaving it here.

Motionless, I waited,
Close yourself, please.

Shouting fell on me,
I saw the alley walker.

He was just a boy, like me,
He must understand.

25

www.ingramcontent.com/pod-product-compliance
Lightning Source LLC
Chambersburg PA
CBHW061328140726
47998CB00007B/2594